What I want to Say To

Shitty Man

The delightful and Swear Words

Adult Coloring Book

By

S.B. Nozaz

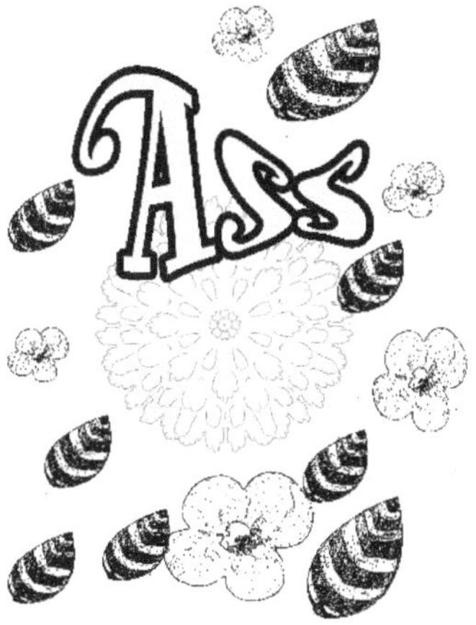

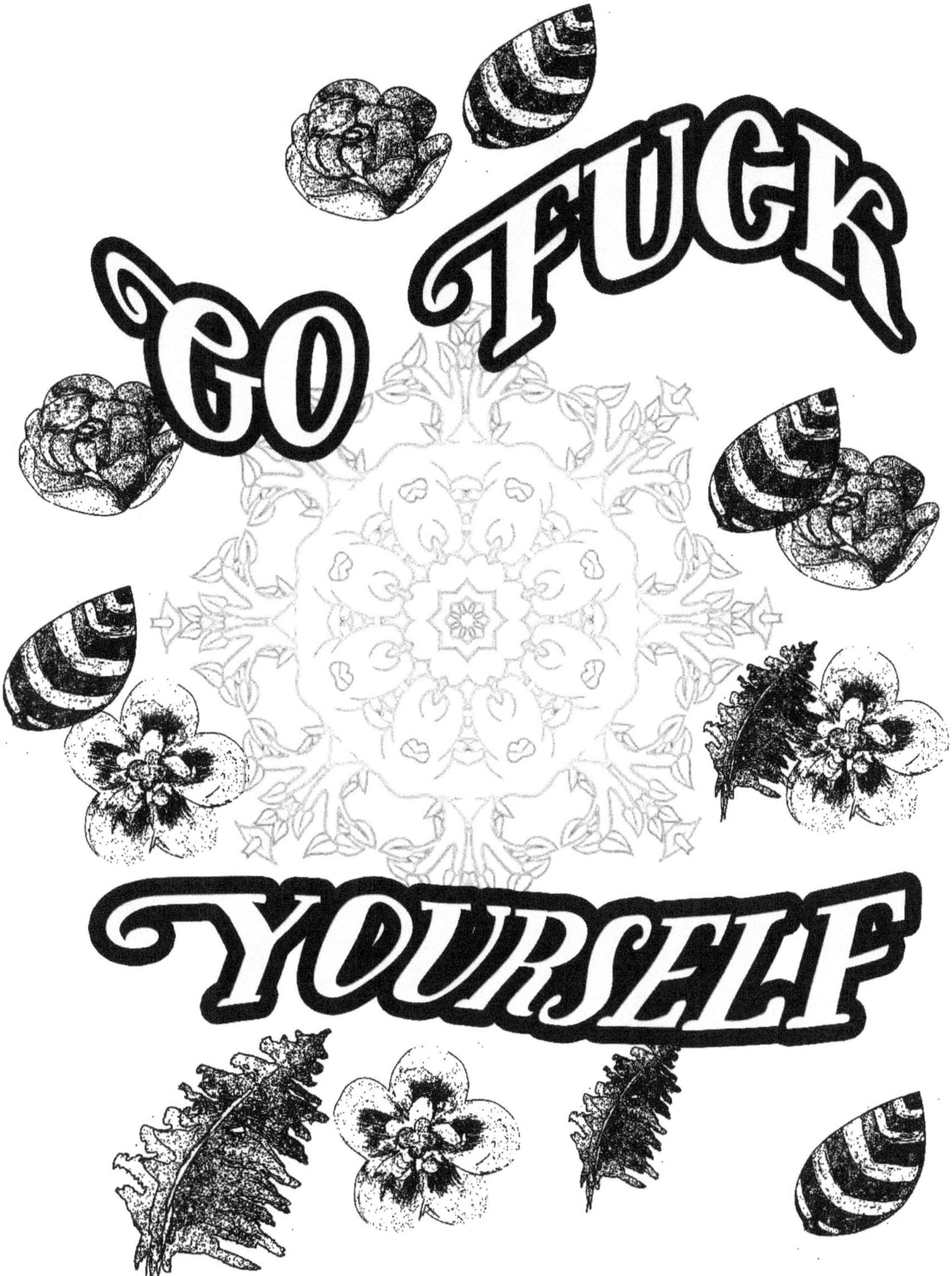
GO FUCK
YOURSELF

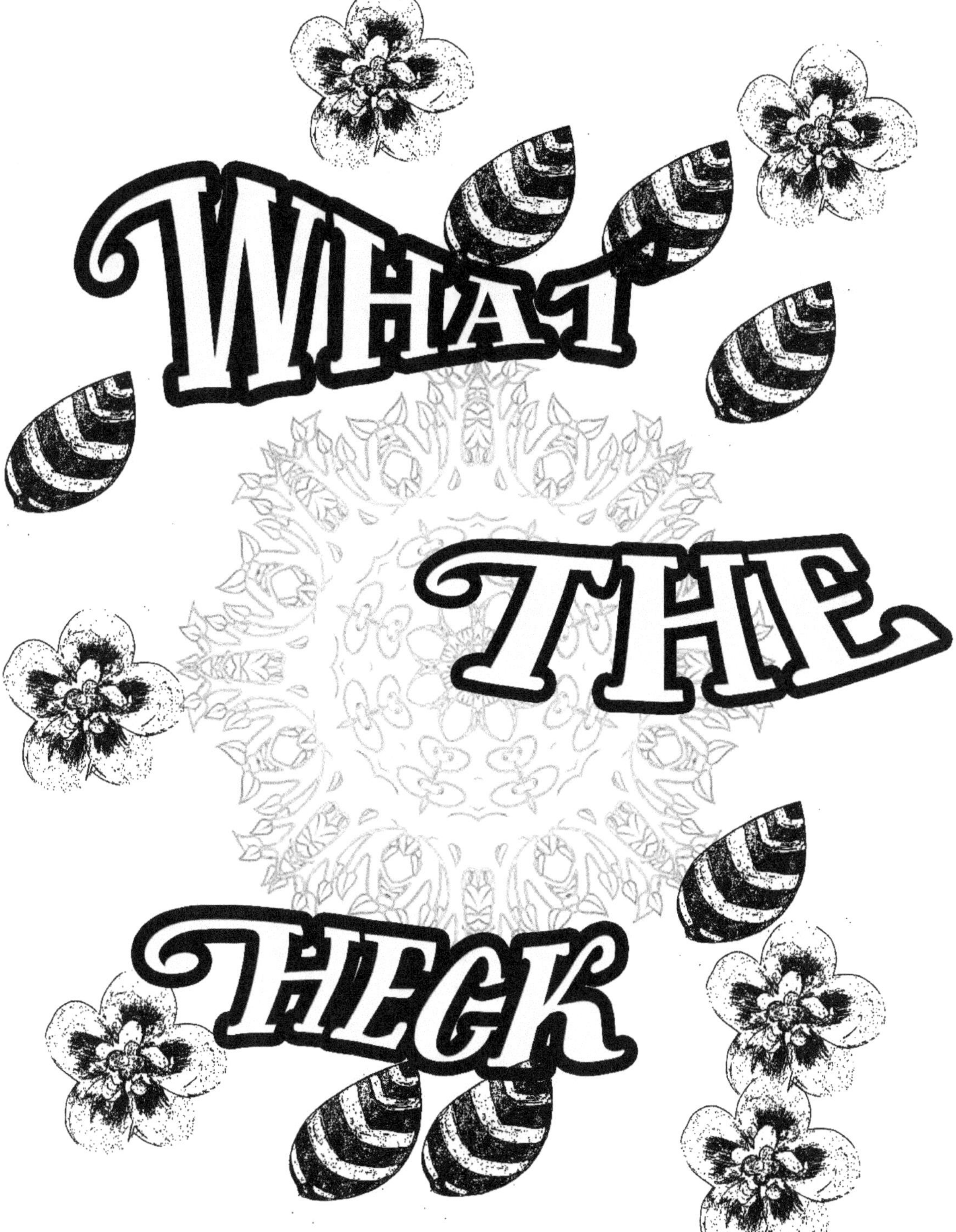
WHAT
THE
HECK

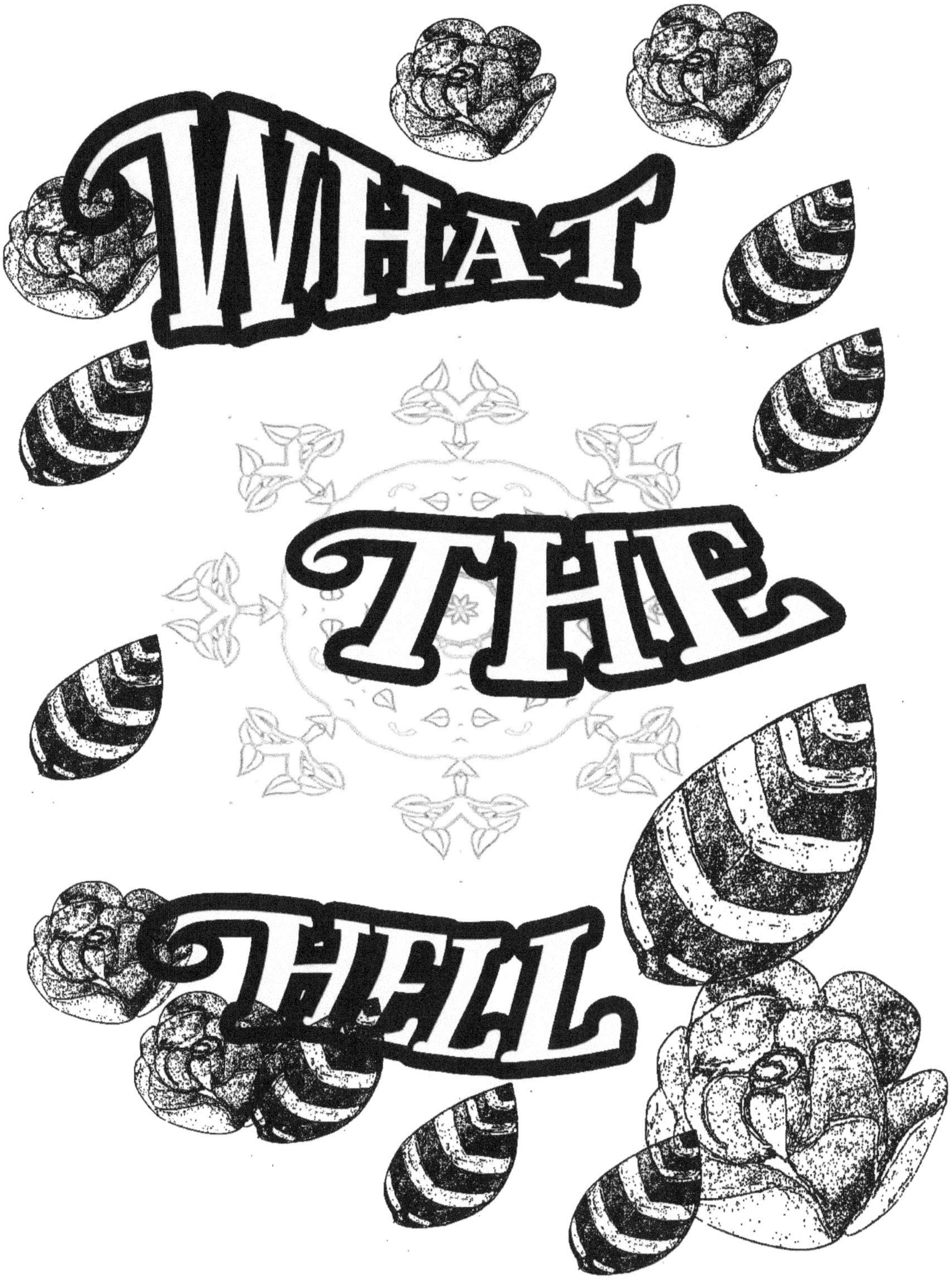
WHAT
THE
HELL

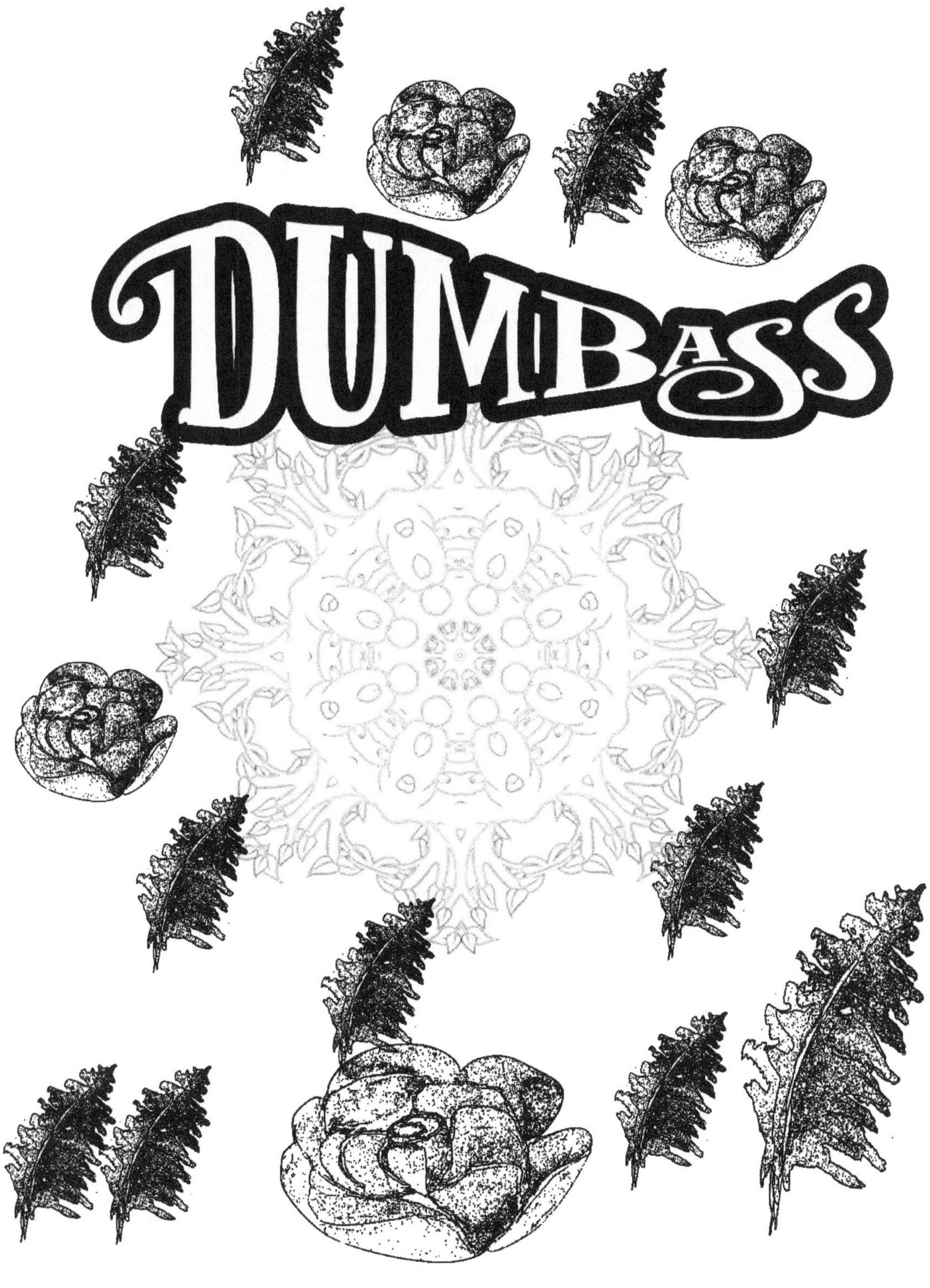
DUMBASS

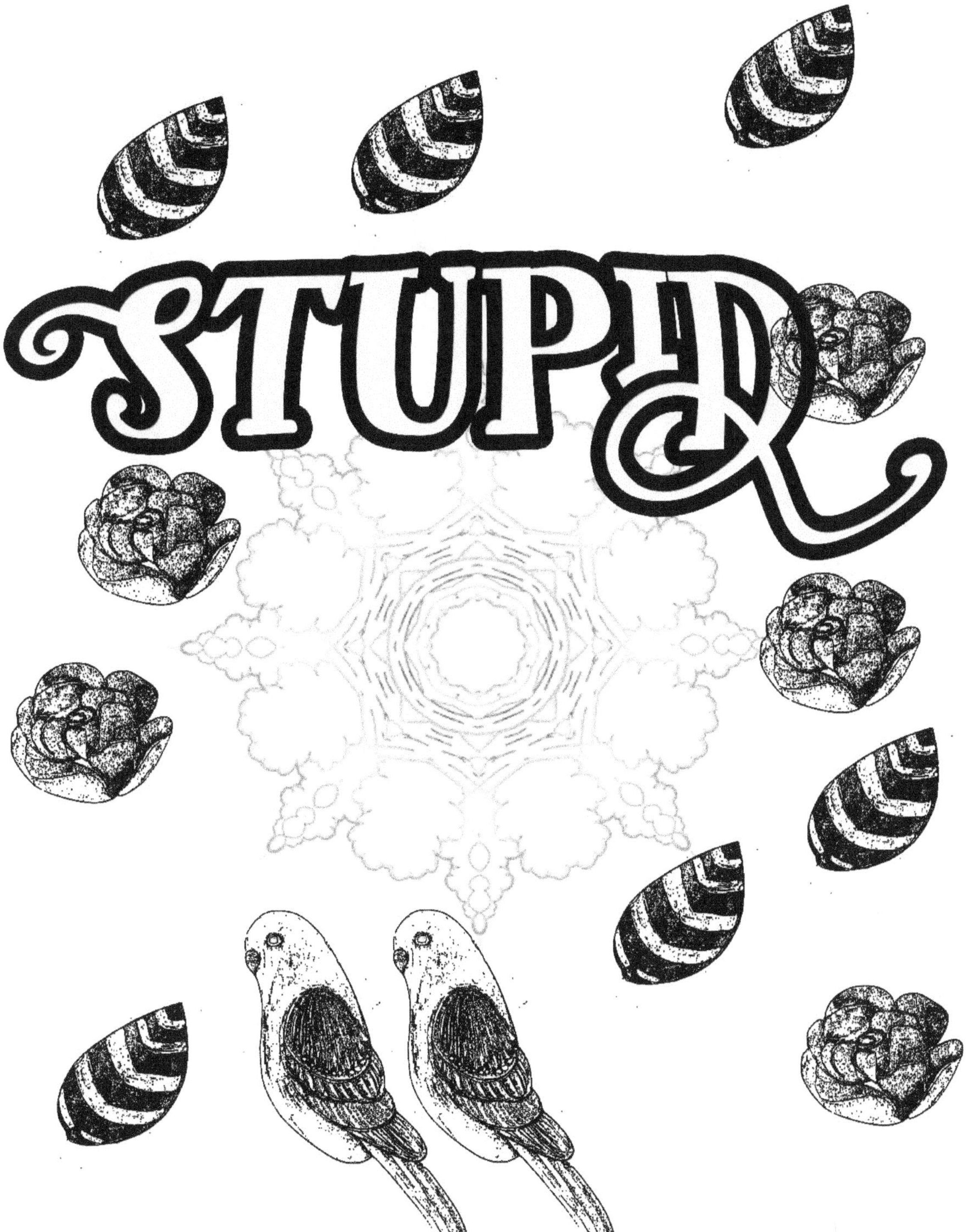
STUPID

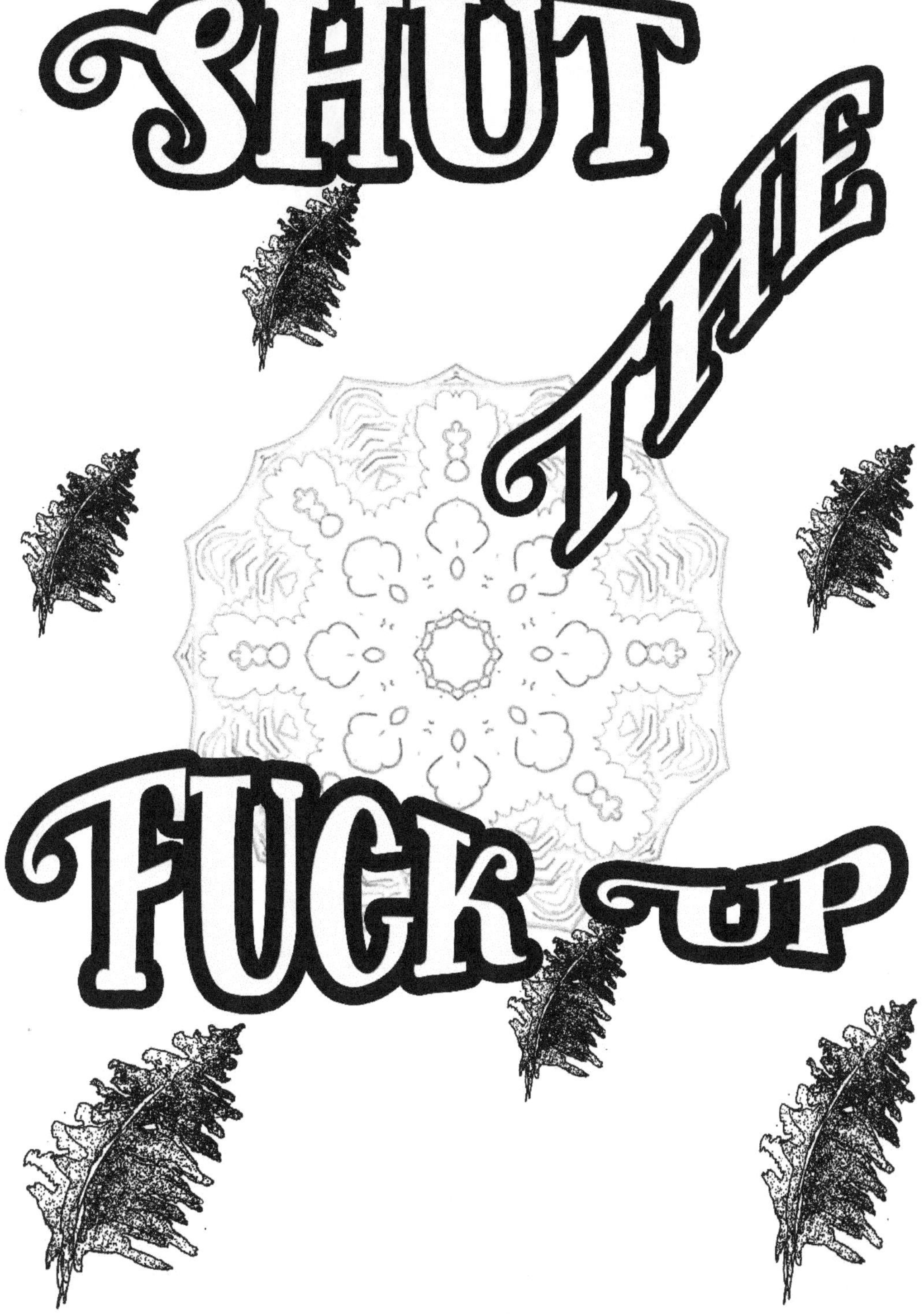
SHUT
THE
FUCK
UP

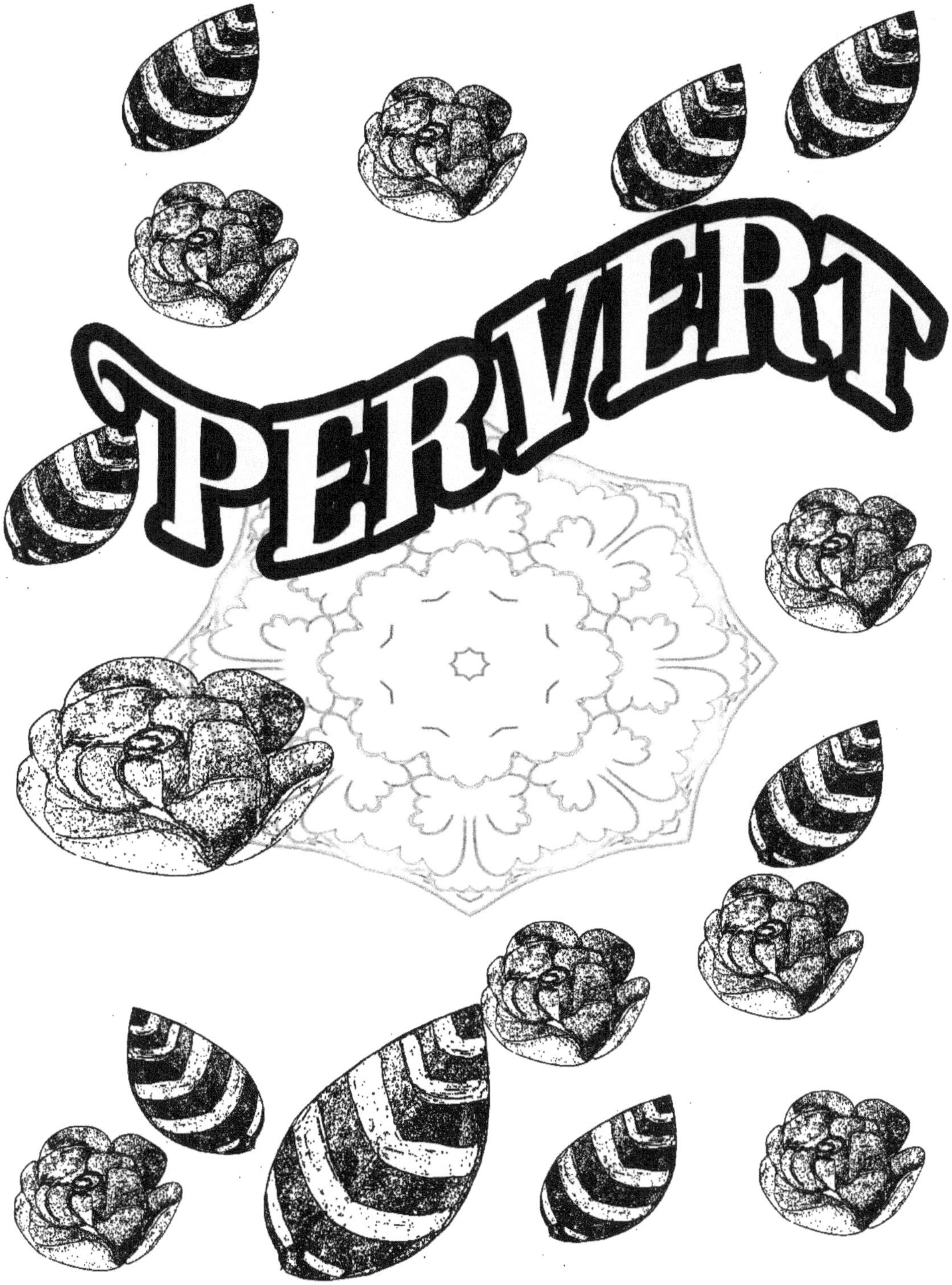
PERVERT

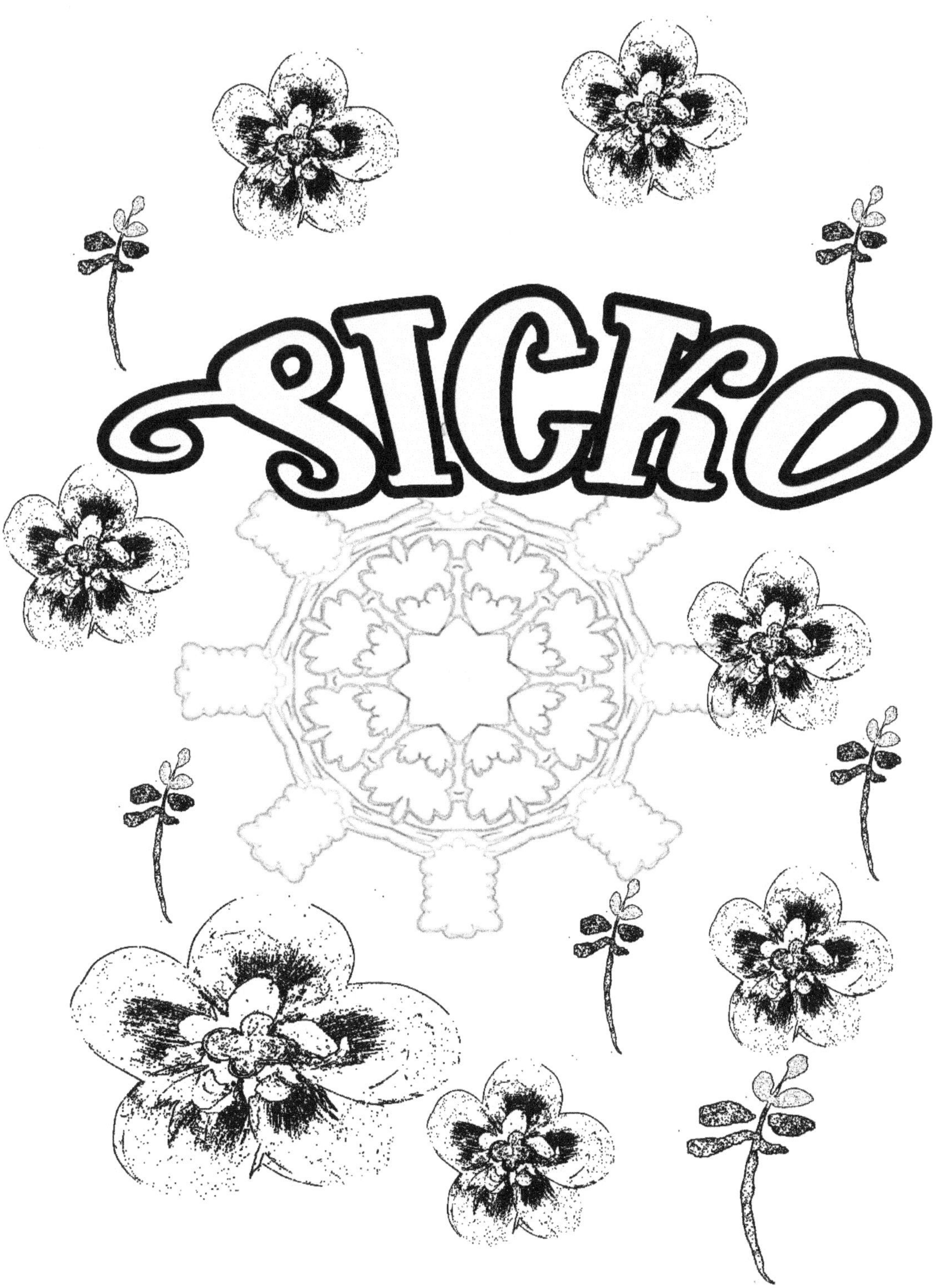
SICKO

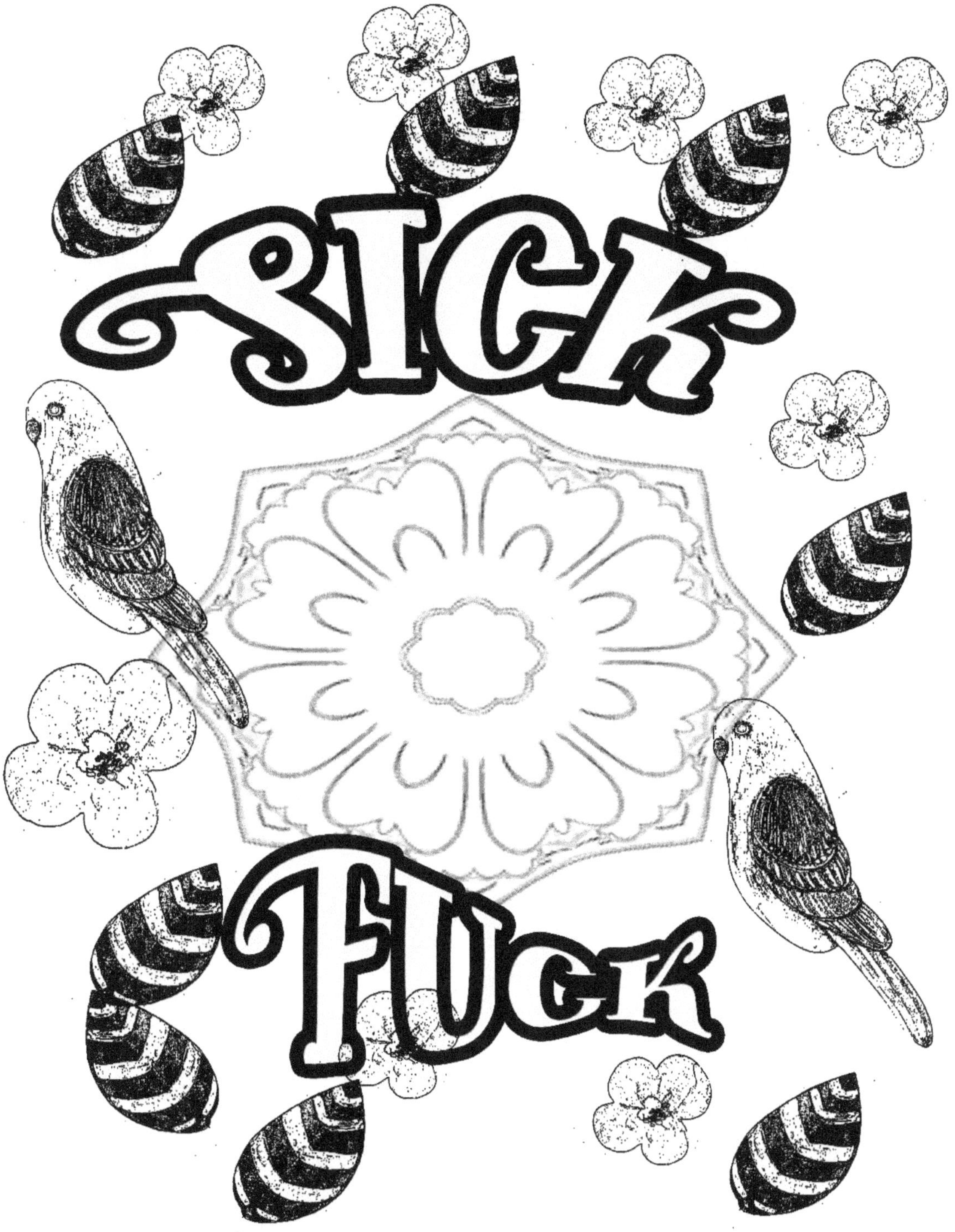
SICK
FUCK

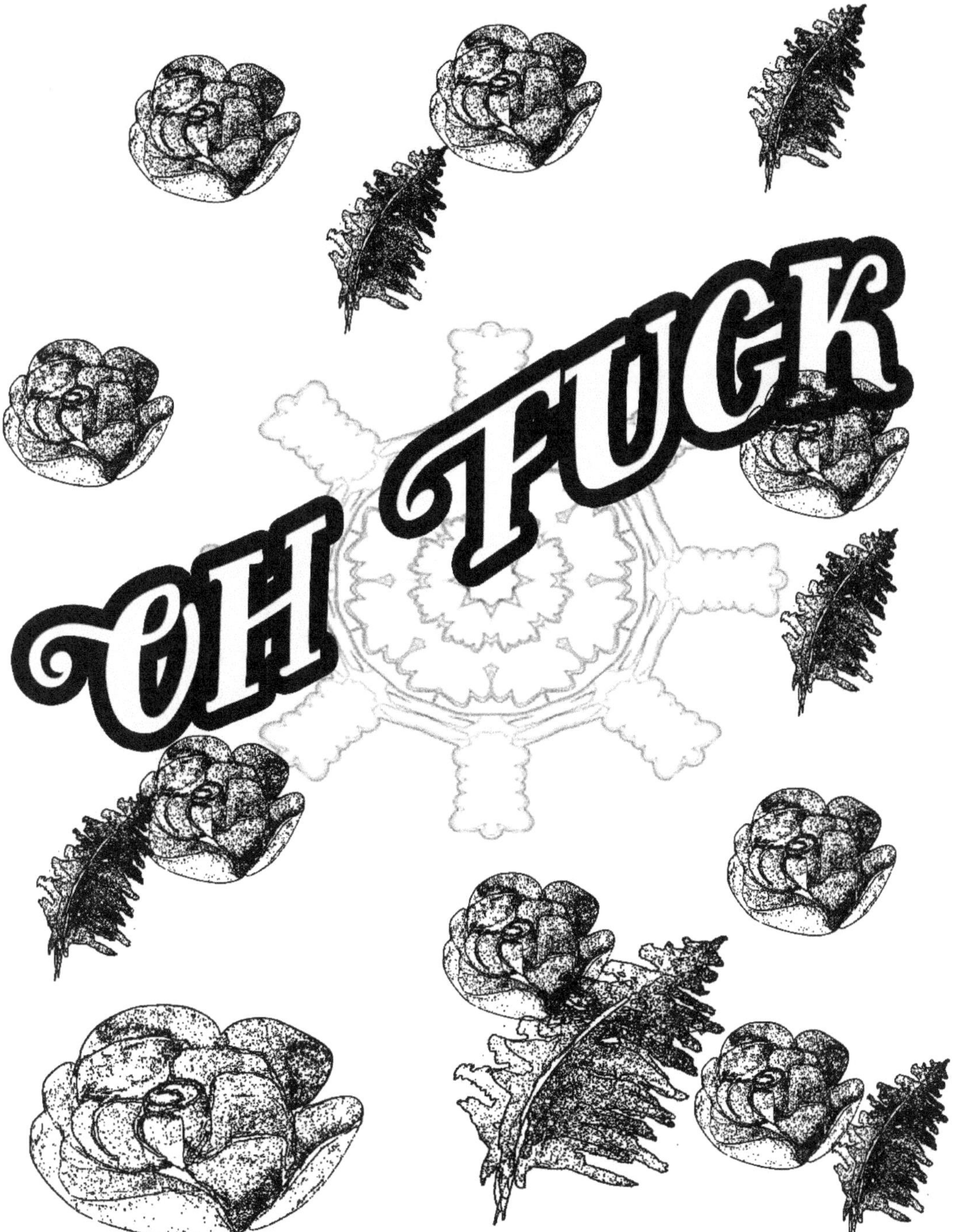
OH FUCK

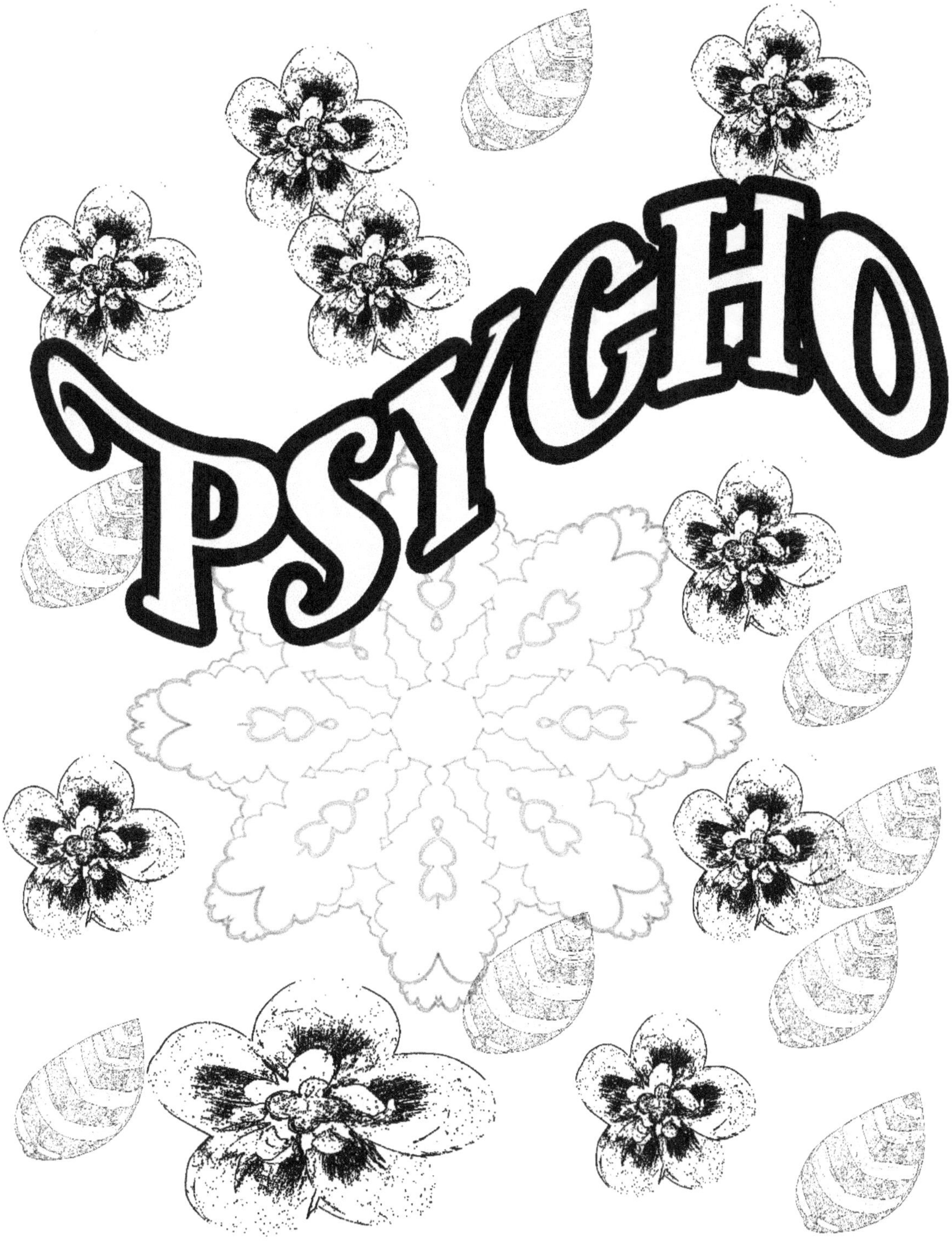
PSYCHO

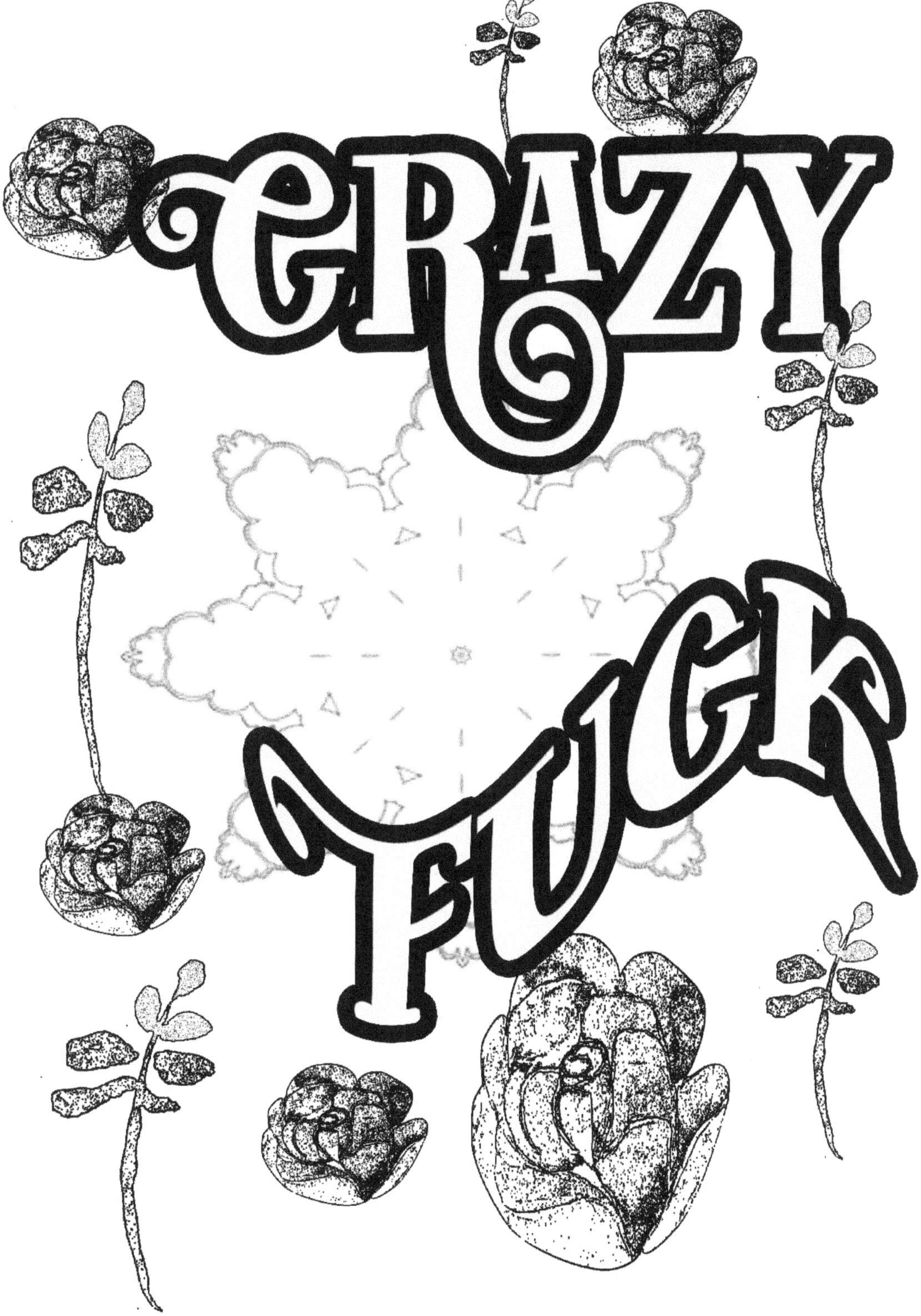
CRAZY
FUCK

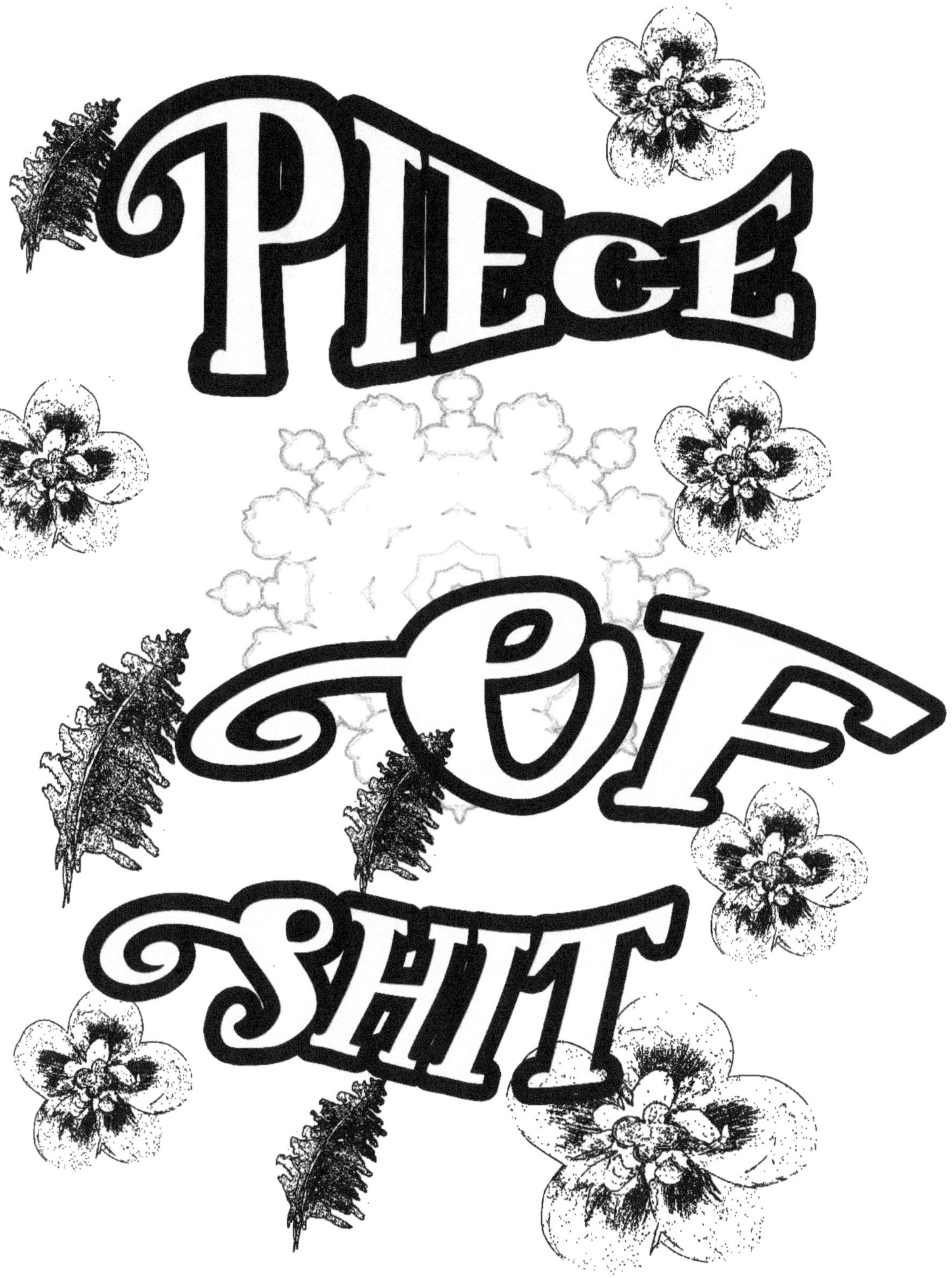
PIECE
OF
SHIT

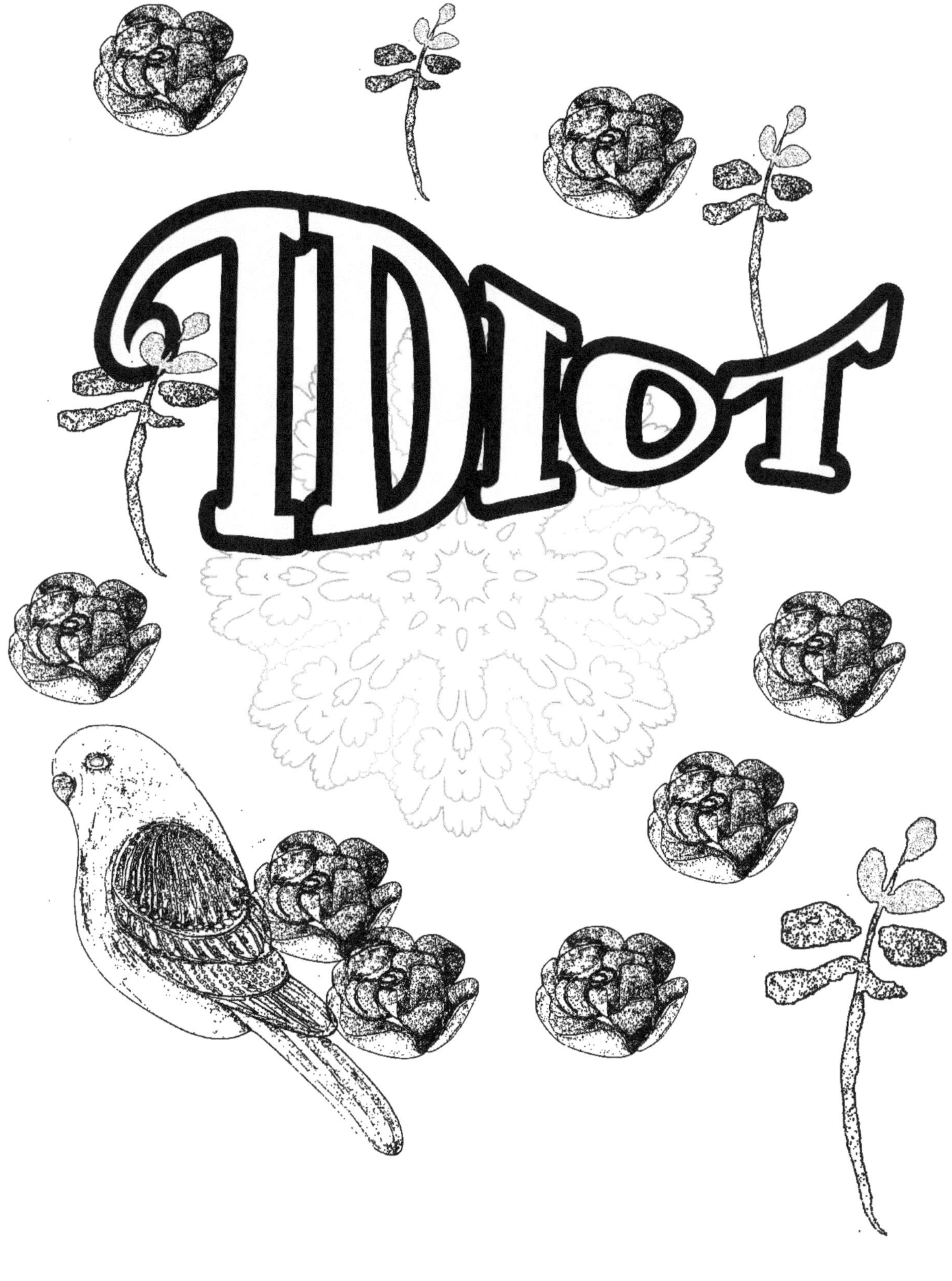
IDIOT

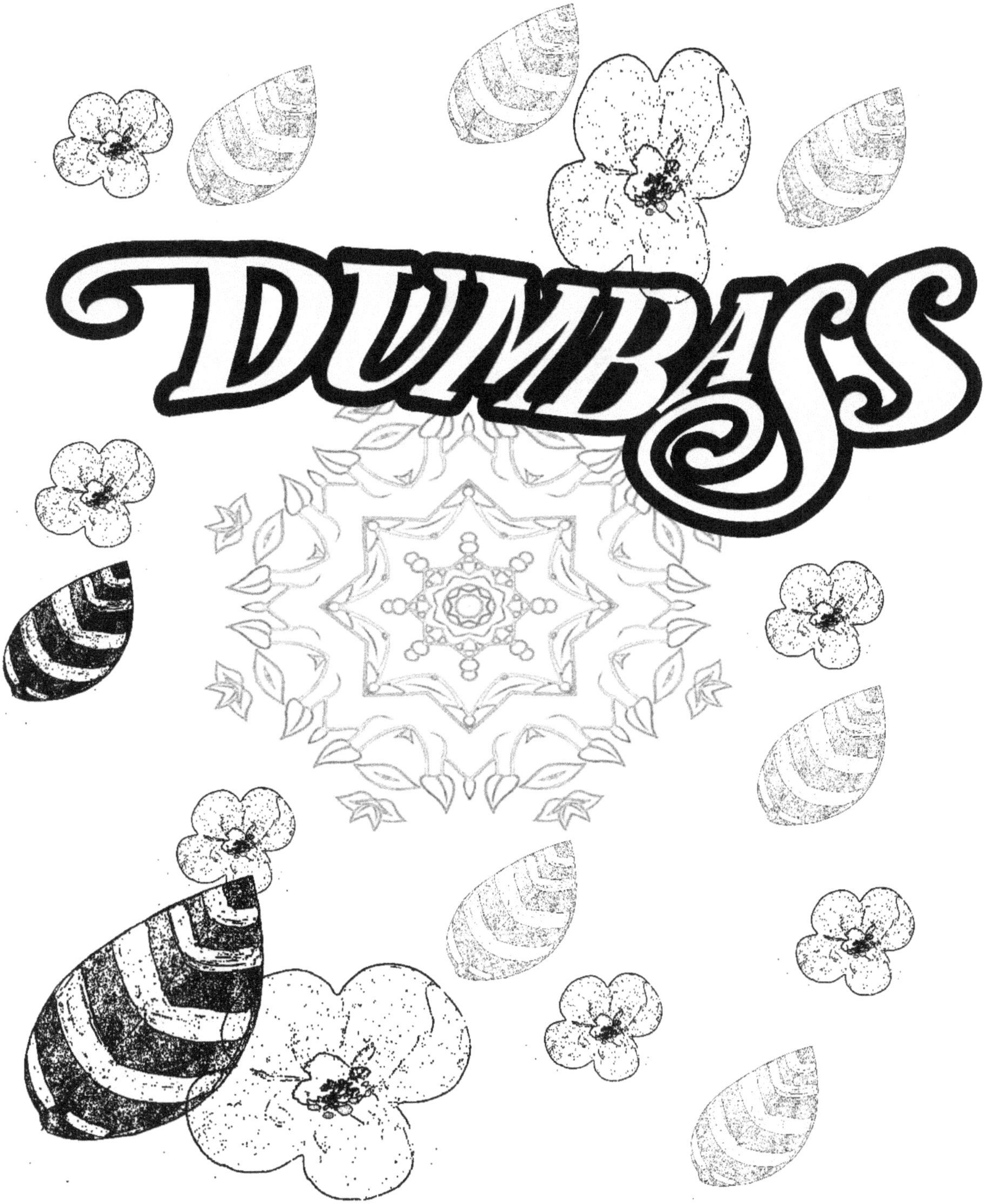
DUMBASS

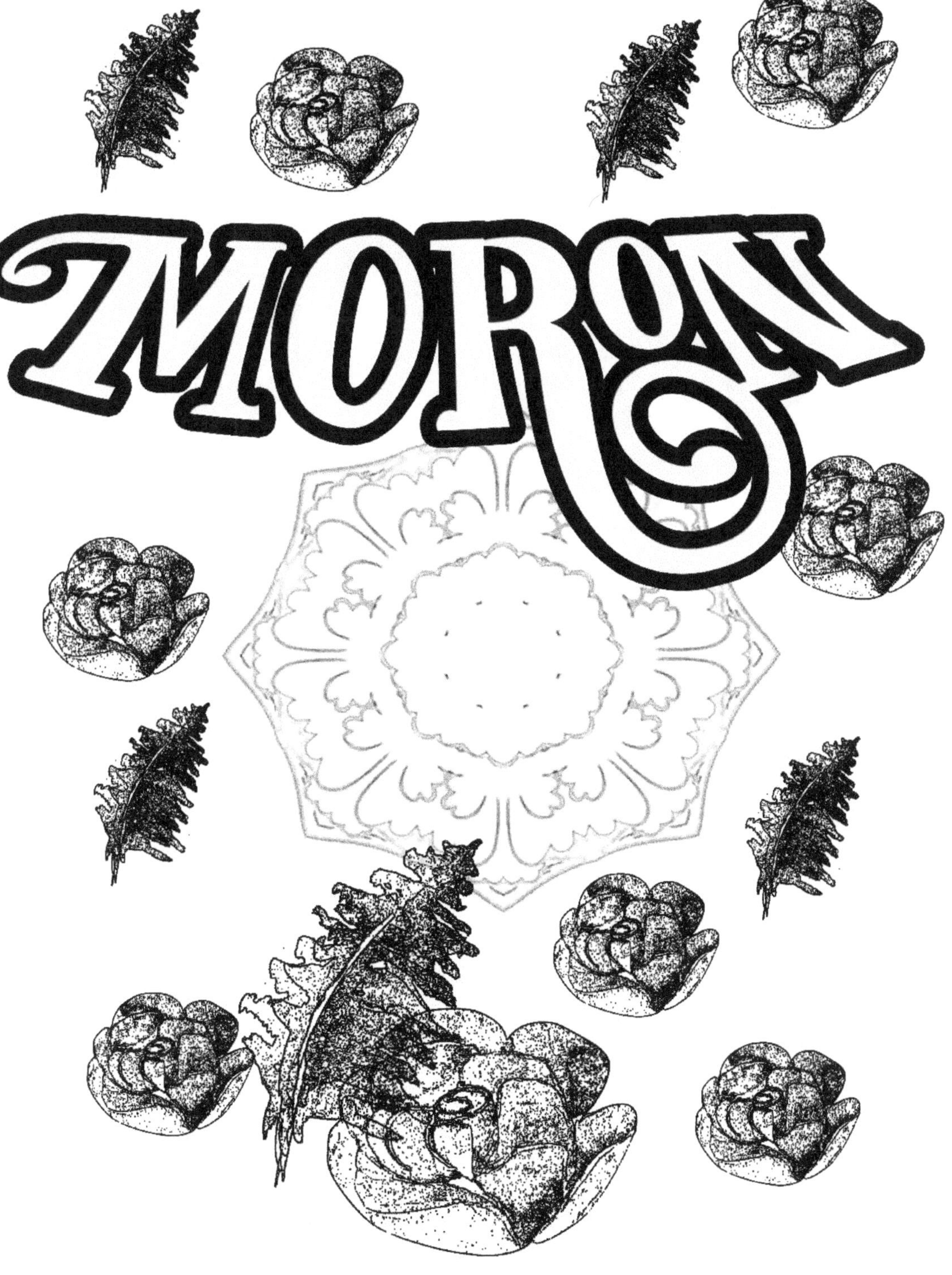
MORON

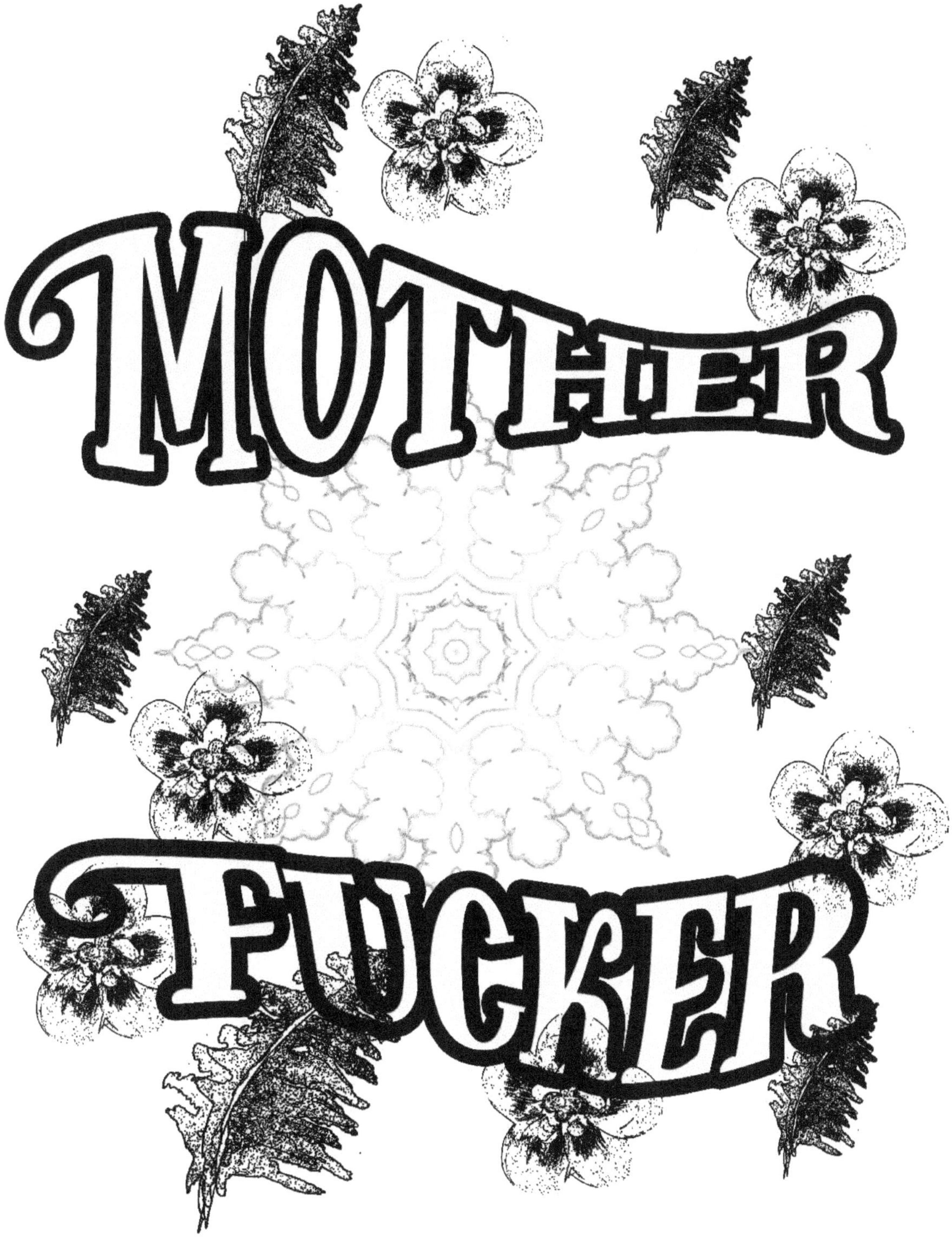
MOTHER
FUCKER

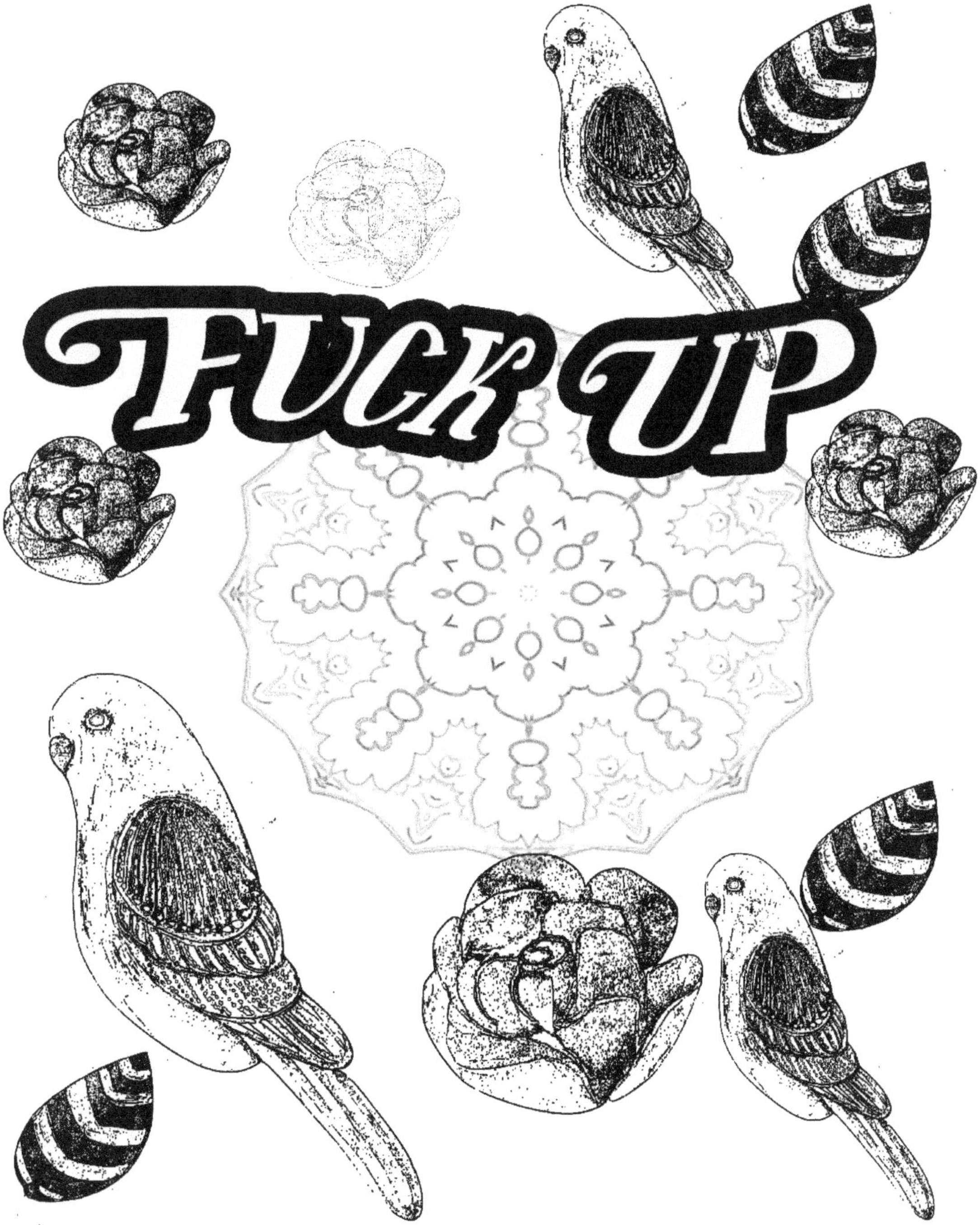
FUCK UP

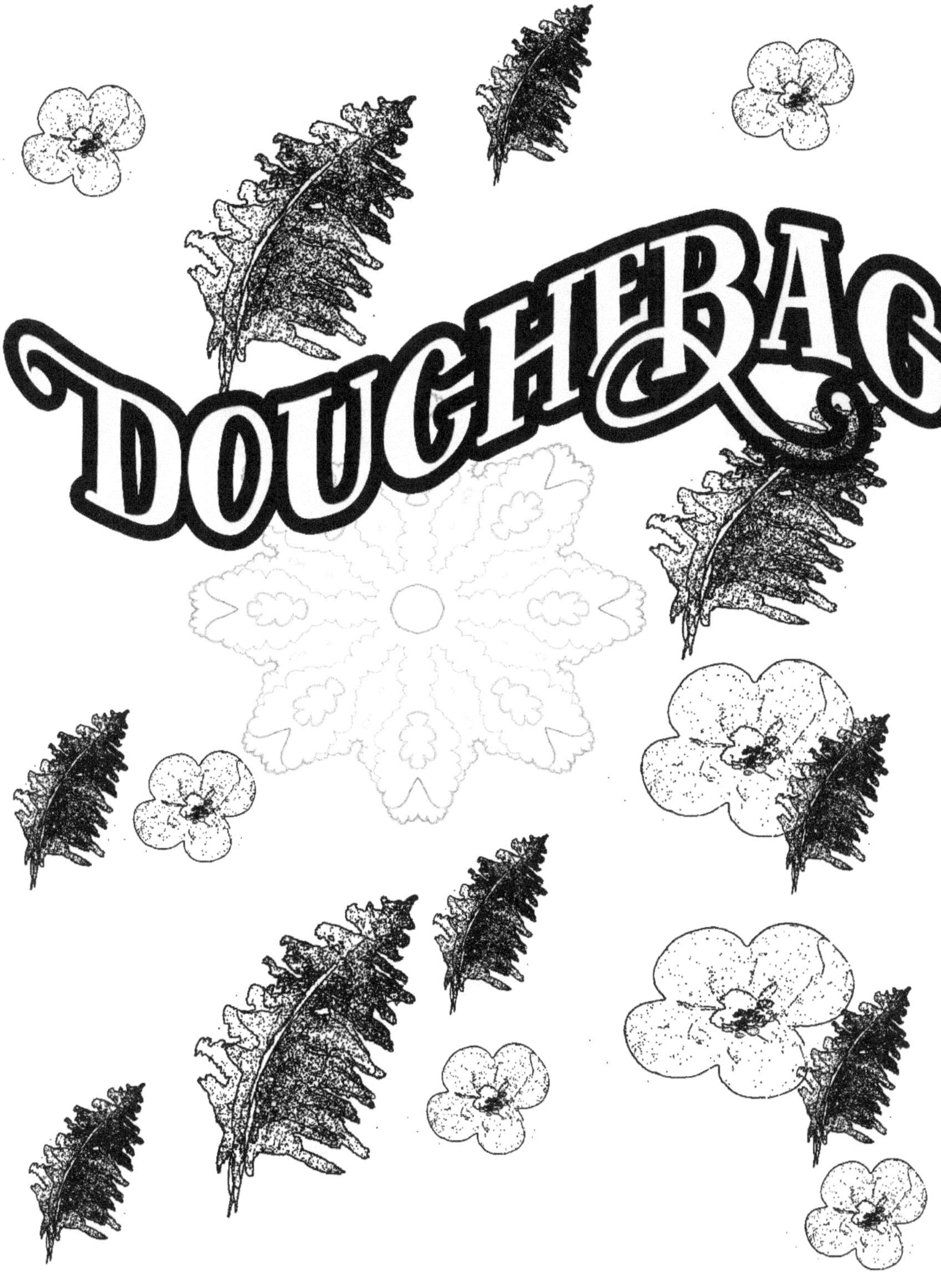
DOUGHEBAG

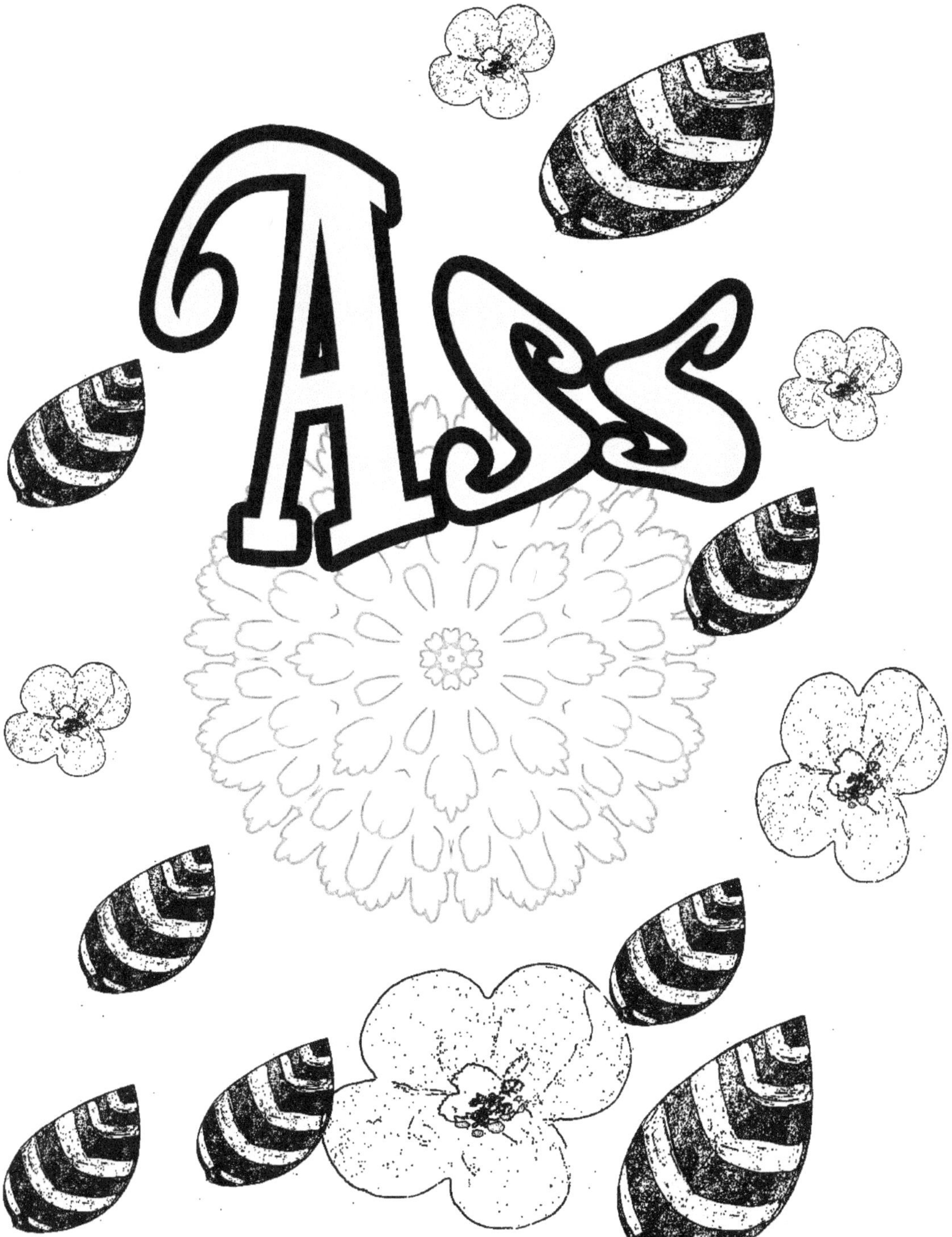
Ass

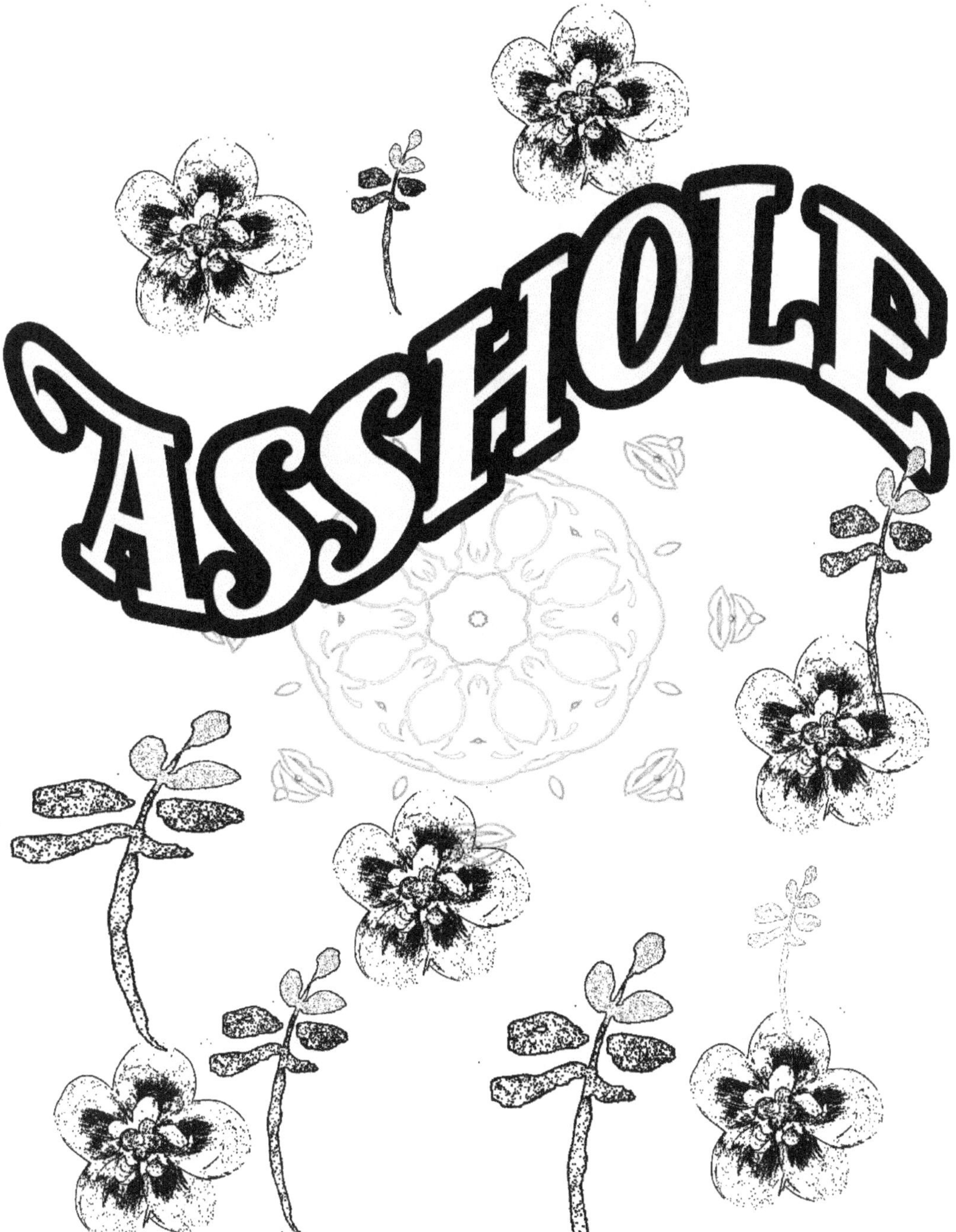
ASSHOLE

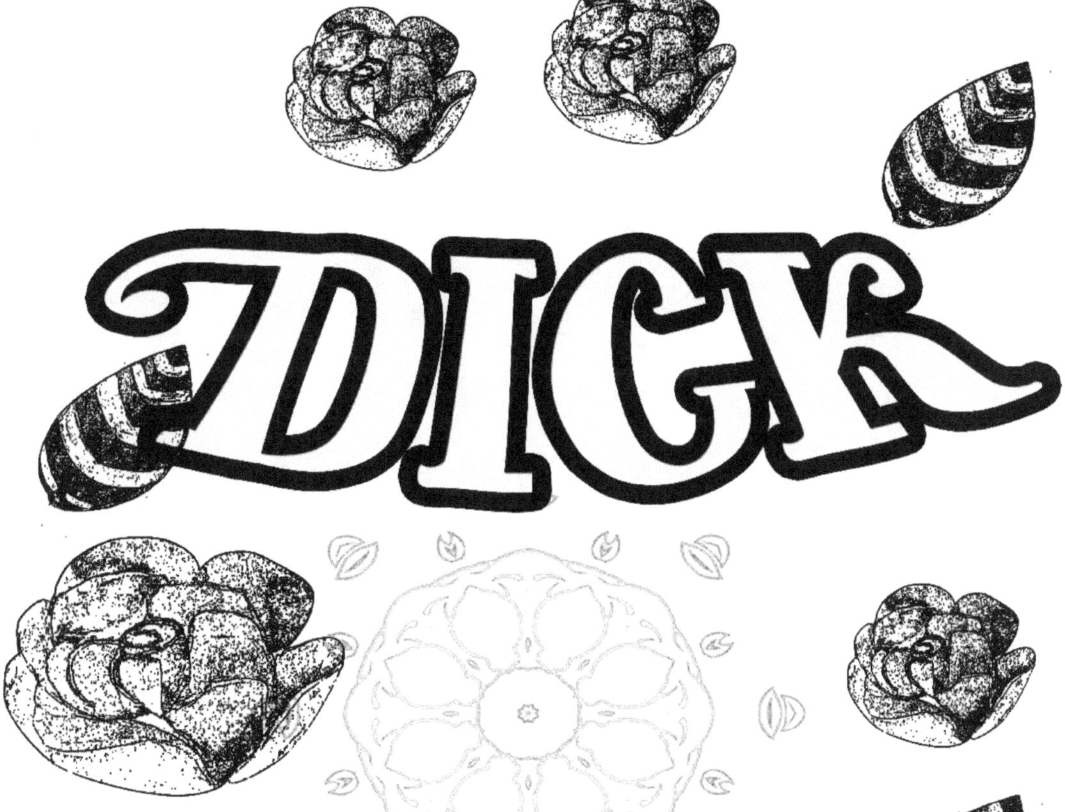
DICK

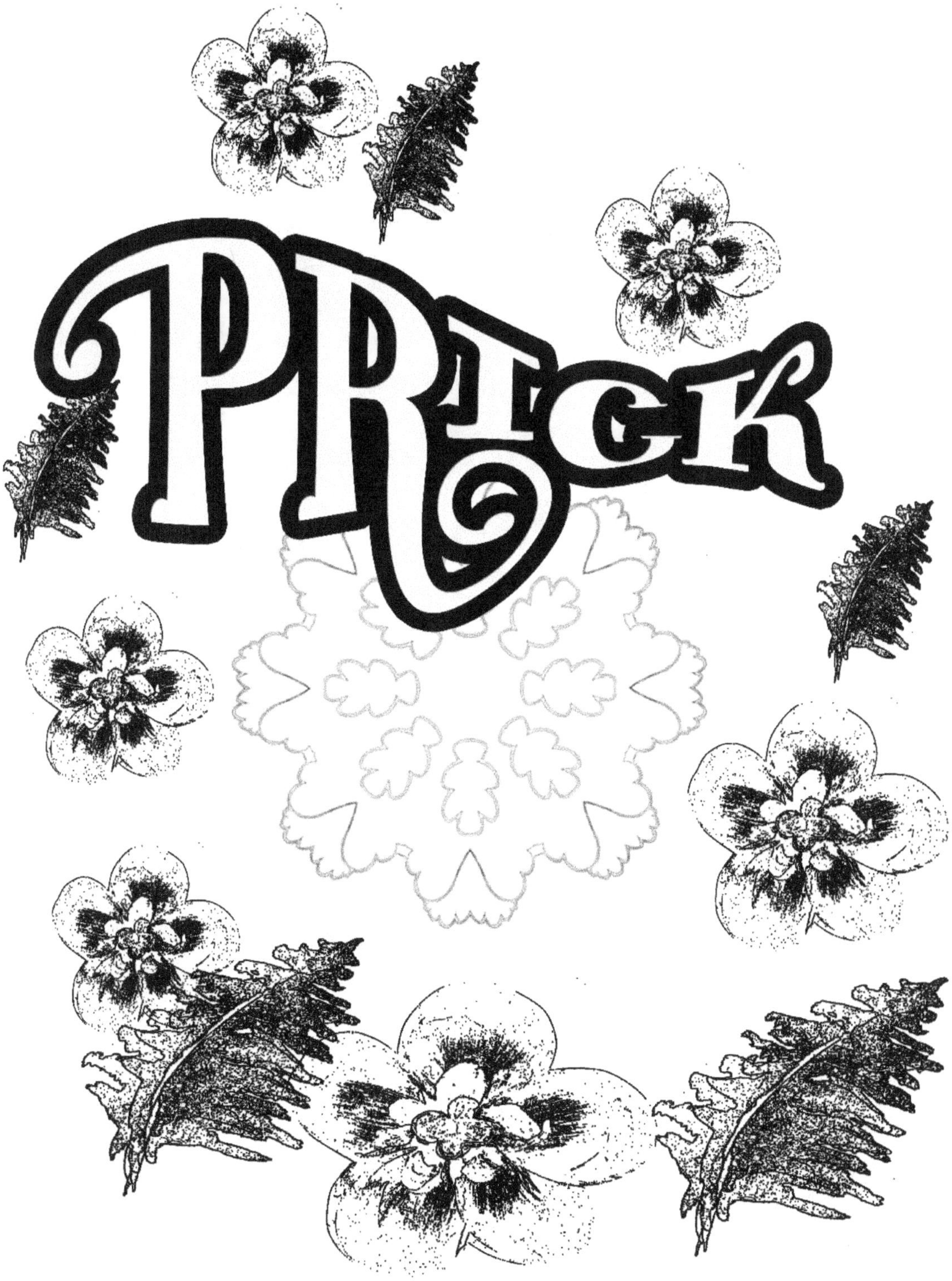
PRICK

Note

www.ingramcontent.com/pod-product-compliance
Lightning Source LLC
Chambersburg PA
CBHW080642190526
45169CB00009B/3462
* 9 7 8 1 5 3 3 2 2 7 0 8 9 *